Garden Room Style

Garden

Room

Style

Peter Marston

RIZZOLI
NEW YORK

First published in the United States
of America in 1998 by
RIZZOLI INTERNATIONAL
PUBLICATIONS, INC.
300 Park Avenue South,
New York, NY 10010

First published in Great Britain in 1998 by
George Weidenfeld & Nicolson Limited
The Orion Publishing Group
Orion House
5 Upper St Martin's Lane
London WC2H 9EA

ISBN 0-8478-2153-6
LC 98-66582

Art Director: David Rowley
Designed by Mark Vernon-Jones
Typeset in Bulmer
Printed in Italy

ACKNOWLEDGEMENTS
This book would not have been possible
without the contribution of numerous
photographers, especially Robin
Matthews who worked together with my
wife, Susan Hirsch, to produce many
outstanding pictures. Jackie Williams
typed the manuscript and my secretary,
Maria Cusack, helped organize the
book. – Peter Marston

Catalogues for Marston & Langinger
conservatories and garden room
furnishings may be ordered by phone:
+44 (0) 171 823 6829

Or visit the website:
http://www.marston-and-langinger.com

Contents

Introduction 6

1 Evolution of garden rooms 8

2 Elements of garden room style 14

3 A leafy perspective 28

4 Decorative elements 48

5 Architectural elements 96

6 Accessories 116

7 Using the garden room 144

Suppliers' addresses 156

Index 158

Introduction

This book is about creating a marriage of house and garden. It is about extending the scents, colours, textures and sounds of outdoors inside, and taking the social and family life of the home, eating and entertaining, out of doors. Garden rooms, with their large windows, doors opening onto the terrace or garden, high roofs and bold architectural features, can be strikingly different to the rest of the home. The construction, even if in traditional style, is an essentially modern concept, with large areas of glass replacing solid walls to let in light and a sense of the garden outside. Over time, garden rooms have developed a distinct style using the structural elements of the building, and textures of stone, brick and stucco, combined with the natural world of plants and flowers, the sun and the stars. Garden rooms offer an environment both stylish and practical, for a relaxed way of living suited to contemporary life.

It is an important room for me, and I have always had a conservatory on my various houses, sometimes small, sometimes large, but usually close to the kitchen. For me, the garden room is also a place in which to work at home peacefully, surrounded by the things I love.

1

Evolution of garden rooms

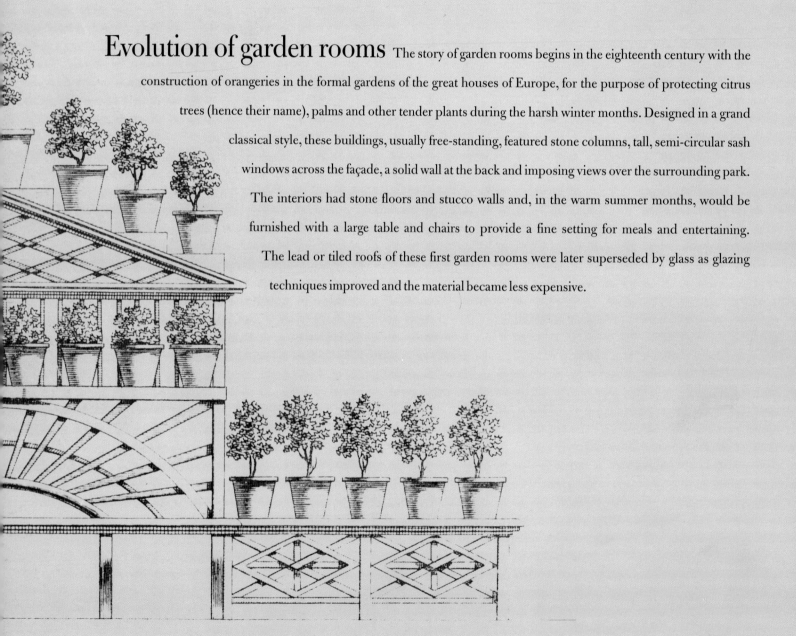

The story of garden rooms begins in the eighteenth century with the construction of orangeries in the formal gardens of the great houses of Europe, for the purpose of protecting citrus trees (hence their name), palms and other tender plants during the harsh winter months. Designed in a grand classical style, these buildings, usually free-standing, featured stone columns, tall, semi-circular sash windows across the façade, a solid wall at the back and imposing views over the surrounding park. The interiors had stone floors and stucco walls and, in the warm summer months, would be furnished with a large table and chairs to provide a fine setting for meals and entertaining. The lead or tiled roofs of these first garden rooms were later superseded by glass as glazing techniques improved and the material became less expensive.

By the following century, glass buildings were being used to house plants throughout the year, leading to the development of iron conservatories – often of monumental proportions. Splendid examples of this architectural form include the Palm House at Kew, completed by Decimus Burton and Richard Turner in 1848, and the enormous Crystal Palace Exhibition Hall by Joseph Paxton, constructed at great speed for the 1851 Trade Fair. In Victorian England this style was adopted on a domestic scale in elaborate confections of glass, wood and cast-iron, richly decorated with brackets, columns and braces, finials, crestings, coloured glass and a lacework of window panes. These conservatories, built onto the homes of the prosperous middle class, were filled with exotic tender plants from the colonies – palms, tree ferns, aspidistras, begonias, orchids – all expensively maintained with coal-fired stoves. Interiors, typically furnished with statuary, ponds and fountains, and staging packed with plants, had less space for people than the earlier orangeries – perhaps just a small marble-topped table and a few chairs for afternoon gossip amongst the tropical flora.

Elements of garden room style

The fundamental, essential, ingredient of a garden room is plants, regardless of whether the room is used as a conservatory, family room, poolhouse or workroom. For those with space, and enthusiasm, indoor plants add a year-round dimension to gardening, and there is a vast and exciting choice of subjects to grow. The two-volume *Conservatory Plants* by Roger Phillips and Martyn Rix, published by Macmillan in London, is a comprehensive and inspirational guide to the planting possibilities. The majority of people, however, have neither the space nor the time for serious conservatory gardening, and, in any case, many plants require humidity and temperatures incompatible with non-gardening use. Instead, there are many plants, especially those of Mediterranean origin, which can thrive in the climate and conditions of a garden room, whether climbers, bulbs, shrubs in containers or plants in pots brought indoors while they are in flower and at their best.

Opposite *The orangery at Iford, Wiltshire, in a 1930's garden by H.A. Peto, who was much influenced by old Italian gardens. Despite the reclaimed-stone classicism of the façade, this building has a modest scale, with a low glass roof barely visible behind the parapet: the design could equally suit a town house and garden. Open to the public.*

Above *The gardens at Alton Towers. While the rest of the conservatory retains the formality of an eighteenth-century orangery, the roof sprouts a fantasy of cast-iron and glass domes. When built, the interior would have been furnished with a formal arrangement of potted plants and iron furniture. Open to the public.*

Above A riot of colour in a mid-century planting scheme still maintained by the gardeners at Glenbervie. The intention here is to make a bold display and provide a supply of potted plants for the house.

By 1900, glass, which a hundred years earlier had been a costly handmade product, was being mass-produced, and glass-and-timber conservatories were now available to almost anyone who could afford their own home. Usually furnished with chequer-pattern tiled floors, wicker furniture from Madeira and the far east, and potted palms in brightly coloured Doulton jardinières, the conservatory became an additional sitting room for leisurely household activities. The First World War marked the end of this way of life, and with it the pursuits symbolised by garden rooms.

Although the conservatories built over the past twenty years have been constructed in the style of the last century, they have been adapted to incorporate large doors which can be folded back in summer to create a link between house and garden, a function absent in Victorian conservatories, which were not designed to provide access to the garden. Thus contemporary conservatories are being used in the manner of the eighteenth-century orangeries – as a place to dine and entertain under glass within view of the garden.

Above *The delicate, glazed, dark-green framework of this Marston & Langinger conservatory encapsulates the room while retaining a strong sense of the garden that surrounds the building. The plants inside, and the low-key furnishings, accentuate this feeling, while the colour scheme, the warm terracotta floor and the snug double glazing ensure that the conservatory is inviting in winter.*

The plants outside – overhanging trees, climbers growing up the side of the garden room, even the general view of the garden – will contribute to the sense of the indoor plant life.

The selection of plants, the particular greens of their foliage, the way in which they grow, the leaf-shape and texture, will all influence the colours and style of the room. But scent is also important and is provided not only by flowers – jasmine, lilies, stephanotis, gardenia (it is usually white flowers that are most perfumed) – but also by scented leaves, herbs, and the many varieties of geraniums. Throughout the year, my own favourites, ginger and cardamom, give off a wonderful perfume when brushed. Oil burners and candles scented with natural oils such as lemon verbena can be added for a special occasion, but cheap chemically-scented candles should be avoided.

***Above** This conservatory doubles as an aviary – a cockatoo and budgerigar are just visible. The Victorian conservatory, built onto the roof top, adjoins the apartment and is used for reading, breakfast, and, when there is time, afternoon tea. The birds look forward to the leftovers.*
***Below** The bright space of a conservatory can be precious in a dark house. Here, plants packed in baskets on the floor, on the window sill, in a wire jardinière, and hanging from the wall, surround the furniture and a china-filled cabinet.*

ELEMENTS OF GARDEN ROOM STYLE

Opposite The orangery at
Iford, Wiltshire, in a 1930's
garden by H.A. Peto, who was
much influenced by old
Italian gardens. Despite the
reclaimed-stone classicism of
the façade, this building has a
modest scale, with a low glass
roof barely visible behind the
parapet: the design could
equally suit a town house and
garden. Open to the public.

Above The gardens at Alton
Towers. While the rest of the
conservatory retains the
formality of an eighteenth-
century orangery, the roof
sprouts a fantasy of cast-iron
and glass domes. When built,
the interior would have been
furnished with a formal
arrangement of potted plants
and iron furniture. Open to
the public.

Above A riot of colour in a
mid-century planting scheme
still maintained by the
gardeners at Glenbervie.
The intention here is to make
a bold display and provide a
supply of potted plants for
the house.

By 1900, glass, which a hundred years earlier had been a costly handmade product, was being mass-produced, and glass-and-timber conservatories were now available to almost anyone who could afford their own home. Usually furnished with chequer-pattern tiled floors, wicker furniture from Madeira and the far east, and potted palms in brightly coloured Doulton jardinières, the conservatory became an additional sitting room for leisurely household activities. The First World War marked the end of this way of life, and with it the pursuits symbolised by garden rooms.

Although the conservatories built over the past twenty years have been constructed in the style of the last century, they have been adapted to incorporate large doors which can be folded back in summer to create a link between house and garden, a function absent in Victorian conservatories, which were not designed to provide access to the garden. Thus contemporary conservatories are being used in the manner of the eighteenth-century orangeries – as a place to dine and entertain under glass within view of the garden.

Above *After an absence of fifty years, conservatories began to reappear as sun rooms with low-pitched roofs, similar to the one shown here, finished with cane furniture, rough matting, house plants and coy sculpture.*
Below *A typical, modern conservatory with a terracotta floor, pine table, simple antiques, pinoleum blinds and a mix of plants and furniture.*

2

Elements of garden room style

The fundamental, essential, ingredient of a garden room is plants, regardless of whether the room is used as a conservatory, family room, poolhouse or workroom. For those with space, time and enthusiasm, indoor plants add a year-round dimension to gardening, and there is a vast and exciting choice of subjects to grow. The two-volume *Conservatory Plants* by Roger Phillips and Martyn Rix, published by Macmillan in London, is a comprehensive and inspirational guide to the planting possibilities. The majority of people, however, have neither the space nor the time for serious conservatory gardening, and, in any case, many plants require humidity and temperatures incompatible with non-gardening use. Instead, there are many plants, especially those of Mediterranean origin, which can thrive in the climate and conditions of a garden room, whether climbers, bulbs, shrubs in containers or plants in pots brought indoors while they are in flower and at their best.

Above *The delicate, glazed, dark-green framework of this Marston & Langinger conservatory encapsulates the room while retaining a strong sense of the garden that surrounds the building. The plants inside, and the low-key furnishings, accentuate this feeling, while the colour scheme, the warm terracotta floor and the snug double glazing ensure that the conservatory is inviting in winter.*

The plants outside – overhanging trees, climbers growing up the side of the garden room, even the general view of the garden – will contribute to the sense of the indoor plant life.

The selection of plants, the particular greens of their foliage, the way in which they grow, the leaf-shape and texture, will all influence the colours and style of the room. But scent is also important and is provided not only by flowers – jasmine, lilies, stephanotis, gardenia (it is usually white flowers that are most perfumed) – but also by scented leaves, herbs, and the many varieties of geraniums. Throughout the year, my own favourites, ginger and cardamom, give off a wonderful perfume when brushed. Oil burners and candles scented with natural oils such as lemon verbena can be added for a special occasion, but cheap chemically-scented candles should be avoided.

Above This conservatory doubles as an aviary – a cockatoo and budgerigar are just visible. The Victorian conservatory, built onto the roof top, adjoins the apartment and is used for reading, breakfast, and, when there is time, afternoon tea. The birds look forward to the leftovers.
Below The bright space of a conservatory can be precious in a dark house. Here, plants packed in baskets on the floor, on the window sill, in a wire jardinière, and hanging from the wall, surround the furniture and a china-filled cabinet.

ELEMENTS OF GARDEN ROOM STYLE

I designed this large
conservatory for a client who
wanted a room big enough for
entertaining but also cosy for
everyday family use. At one
end we built a fireplace for log
fires, and used warm textures
and rugs. The owners
requested a traditional,
Victorian-looking
conservatory suited to the
architecture of the house, but
with a contemporary
interior. To overcome this
apparent conflict of style, I
did not compromise the

design of the building, but
instead used colour and
texture in the furnishings to
create the look. On the floor is
wild-grained Burgundy
limestone with a thick abaca
rug. The walls are textured
Siena-coloured stucco, and
the woodwork is painted in
warm greys with mushroom-
coloured blinds in the roof.
Over the fireplace is an
antique Saharan fabric, with
bold brass candlesticks. The
hanging baskets are filled
with Spanish moss.

The use of materials usually associated with the outdoors adds to the sense of the garden room. Rough brick, stone and terracotta, which might be inappropriate elsewhere in the house, belong in this environment, as do stuccoed walls and old garden furniture transferred indoors. These materials and textures relate naturally to the plants inside the room, and create a relaxed space compatible with informal living.

Light and colour are fundamental to the concept – I cannot imagine a dark garden room. The lightest garden room of all will be a conservatory-type structure, all glass with a metal or wood frame. Ideally, light should enter through the roof, and even if this is only by means of a lantern roof set into a solid ceiling, this room will still be the brightest one in the house. Alternatively, large windows or glazed doors making a screen on one or more sides of a room (as in the earliest orangeries), have a similar effect and admit a view of the garden or terrace outside. The light, and the proximity of the garden will inevitably influence the particular palette of colours in the room – the greens, earth colours, brick and stone serve as a background to the brilliant colours of flowers, which can be echoed in bright fabrics.

Above A club dining room beneath a stained glass conservatory roof. The walls are decorated with murals showing a Mexican jungle theme, with wild birds and animals.

Below Town conservatories do not always overlook a pretty garden. Here, a passageway outside is decorated with trellis and pots at the top, while linen blinds mask the view of neighbouring walls and soften the lines of the conservatory at eaves level. This very small conservatory (9 sq metres/95 sq ft) has wire and iron furniture, which has the advantage of not appearing bulky in a restricted space.

Opposite The Chinese Room at Langley Park. A room high enough for a balcony, with enormous sash windows and white-painted, Chinese-style furniture creating a bold interior.

Opposite *Poolhouses – the most spectacular way to bring the outdoors inside – need softening touches to make them attractive rooms. Here there are orange trees, plumbago, passion flowers and orchids, long canvas curtains and cushions, carved animal primitives, and tailor-made wicker furniture.*

Above A garden room
attached to a large house in
Pennsylvania. When
furnishing a conservatory,
the roof is often neglected.
Here it is decorated
successfully with swags of
carefully trained creepers.
Below While restoring and
converting a barn, the owners
boldly glazed large sections to
create a full-height oak-and-
glass garden room, making
the most of a framed timber
construction for a bright
sunny room in what
otherwise could have been a
dark building.

An important element of garden rooms is the approach to the architecture. Whereas other rooms in a private house are constructed from brick, steel and concrete with wooden joists covered in insulation, plaster and other materials, in a glass building nothing is hidden: the decoration is the structure and vice-versa.

A further aspect of the garden room's appeal is the seeming contradiction of being close to the outside world and yet insulated from it. This is most apparent in the heated public glass-houses of the nineteenth century – I remember a winter's afternoon in the steaming heat of the Palm House at Kew Gardens just outside London, with a panoramic view of the surrounding park carpeted with deep snow. In a private house, the contrast of temperature will not be so dramatic, but it is always satisfying to be able to sit comfortably indoors within sight of the frost-covered garden. All these elements – light, scent, colour, the closeness to nature, the use of natural materials and honesty of construction, and a relaxed environment – should influence every aspect of the garden room from its construction to the objects that fill it.

Above *A deliberately greenhouse style was used here, with modest-looking, olive-green paintwork to avoid competing with the mellow Cotswold stonework. Inside are comfy sofas and armchairs and plenty of space to relax.*

A conservatory, located in Hamburg, built independent of the house, with its own kitchen and a log fire. The owners wanted to retain a strong sense of the outdoors, and asked for old-brick walls and a floor of antique limestone flags. At the centre is a table long enough to seat sixteen or more, which was put up for a party and never taken down. Because the room is large, different areas are possible: the table in the middle; a cozy spot by the fire; and, farthest from the house, lots of plants, including palms and olive trees.

3

A leafy perspective

The colour, scent, pattern and texture of leaves and flowers are essential elements of garden rooms, whether as a green canopy of overhanging branches dappling the light through a glass roof, a mass of blossoms viewed through the windows and doors, or planting inside in pots. Outside, the most effective planting will be evergreen, especially architectural plants like hardy palms, cordylines, phormium, holly, yew and box, which can be accented by plants with scent and blossom. Inside, plants become a part of the furnishing of the room, contributing to its style and character, whether as a wall of climbers – jasmine, passion flower or stephanotis – or simply delicate spring bulbs in pots. For me, tending plants and watching them grow is an essential activity in the conservatory. I like the simple pleasure, while having breakfast, of seeing new shoots appear on old favourites or discovering for the first time that a new specimen is covered in flower buds.

*Above Steamboat Gothic.
Two storeys of carved and
turned wooden balconies
in Savannah, Georgia.
Apart from the bizarre style
and additional space they
create, balconies such as
this help to keep the house
cool in summer.*
*Below Gardens at Port
Lympne, Kent, built in 1913,
with a garden designed by
Russell Page. The house has
pretty sheltered terraces with
views of the garden below, and
wisteria-clad stone columns
with beautiful ironwork
designed by Philip Tilden.*

Terraces and verandas

Terraces and verandas serve as the transitional areas between house and garden. Verandas grew in popularity during the latter part of the eighteenth century and became a feature of Regency houses. They were built of wood and wrought iron (later cast-iron) in delicate trellis patterns often derived from classical motifs, with copper or lead-covered roofs, usually concave in form. These mostly shallow lean-to structures were built onto a paved terrace, or constructed one storey above, leading off a drawing room. Some were double-storey, and many were later glazed in. As well as being attractive, highly decorative features – especially when covered with wisteria or other trailing plants – verandas also provide protection against the weather, making it possible to leave windows and French doors open in the rain, or to sit under the shade of a canopy on sunny days. New verandas are easily constructed with a wood frame and shaped rafters supporting the roof. If metal coverings are not available or appropriate for the house, small slates are excellent substitutes, and even shingles or small glass panes with scalloped edges can be used.

A terrace leading from the back of the house to the garden provides an intermediate area for benches, chairs and tables, perhaps with an umbrella for shade. The effectiveness of a terrace used as an outside room can be emphasised by partially enclosing the space with hedges, fences or low walls. The combination of a garden room, veranda and terrace, leading perhaps to a barbecue or a pool beyond, provides three auxiliary areas that can be used according to the weather.

Above *A Regency wrought-iron and wood veranda close to Kew Gardens, near London. The slate roof, which could equally well have been gracefully-curved copper, compliments the plumbago-blue paintwork, which in turn is effective against the white stucco. The veranda allowed French doors to be added upstairs for a bright drawing room.*

Left *Sheltered from the ocean behind a glass screen, this terrace is used as an extension to the house for meals outside. There is a nautical feel to the furnishings: blue and white, with a scrubbed-pine table top.*
Opposite *Dramatic canvas shades, which can be slid back out of the way in wet weather and winter. Apart from softening the sunlight, they contain the space on this rooftop terrace to create a garden room, simply furnished.*
Overleaf *The charm of blinds derives from the softening, filtering effect they have on sunlight, accentuated here by the gaps between the curtains that allow the sun to stream across the room, leaving silhouettes on the floor and linen table cloth.*

Opposite *A screen of trellis on the front side encloses this terrace to make a pretty outside room with tables and chairs amongst greenery.*

Above *This rooftop terrace in central London is protected from winds by the surrounding buildings. The terrace is a pleasant spot with views of the neighbouring gardens. Lunch is reached via the adjoining conservatory, and is served from a folding teak table and chairs set with rustic twig table mats and pretty cast-glass goblets. The central flower arrangement reflects the cheerful colour scheme of the furnishings.*

The garden outside A garden room is a room with a view. For most gardeners this will be an opportunity to enjoy unusual plants as they develop, and to watch from close quarters as winter and early-spring flowers come into bud and then blossom. The terrace outside is a good spot for spring bulbs grown in pots, while climbers – wisteria, roses and clematis – can be grown up over a glass roof; the view through glass of a banksia rose in spring, for example, is delightful. Overhanging branches of any nearby established trees will provide an attractive canopy of leaves over the roof, and shade from the summer sun. New buildings need planting around them in the form of climbers, beds, container-plants and trees.

The view of the garden needs to be groomed by growing plants for privacy, trimming or removing existing plants in order to create a vista, or introducing ornamental plants to improve the view. The colours and textures of the chosen plants should be harmonious, and a limited palette of colours is often the most effective.

Top A conservatory leading onto an upstairs terrace, with a wooden deck. Plants include lavender, rosemary and bay for the kitchen, set in attractive terracotta pots.
***Above** The simple year-round city garden has no lawn; instead, pale shingle has been used. It offers an advantage in shade, reflecting the light to make the garden brighter.*

***Opposite** The dark-green paintwork of this classical glasshouse in Lübbecke, Germany blends well with the colours of the garden, which includes a large over-hanging copper beech. Inside there is a strong sense of outdoors, with lots of plants, a brick floor and masses of greenery pressing against the glass.*

Opposite *Next to the house, the lawn gives way to the texture of cobbles, container plants, and climbers against the pretty Gothic windows and iron balcony. A canvas garden umbrella is an attractive way to provide shade.*

Below *Barely visible from close up, the dramatic lantern roof is a surprise on entering the room. Ivy has covered the wall in the four years since the room was constructed, disguising the raw newness of the brick.*

Overleaf *With so much glass, the garden surrounding a conservatory should look good. Here the building was aligned on an existing avenue of pleached limes, and on each side are lawns set with mature trees. I designed this building to be in scale with the manor house that it is built against – parts are medieval with Gothic tracery, which reflects the theme for the architectural embellishments of the conservatory.*

Opposite *A small town garden can be integrated completely with the rest of the home in summer if the garden is reached through large doors that fold back. In the foreground are tomatoes, basil, and mustard seedlings.*

Above *Inside-outside. With the doors folded back the conservatory relates closely with the garden outside. The Yorkstone paving outside is also used inside, but is smooth-finished (covered with an Atlas-mountains tapis de terre rush mat). There are plants and chairs both inside and outside. Evergreen plants have been chosen for the garden, including hardy palms. In the foreground is a bougainvillea set in a rush basket.*

Overleaf *The interior of the new Sensory Garden conservatory I designed for Kew Gardens. The roof is covered with stone-painted pinoleum blinds, and their effect on sunlight can be seen in the patterns projected onto the floor.*

4

Decorative elements

Although garden rooms are dominated by natural light, the decorative elements are equally important. Without the utility created by a good colour scheme, appropriate furniture, lighting, plants and accessories, the room will lack appeal and therefore, unless it is an essential living area, will be little used. Furnishing a garden room is an opportunity to enjoy using ideas and furniture that could not be used elsewhere in the house. Conventional furnishing ideas – either spare drawing room minimalism, or heavily upholstered pieces, mahogany and elaborate curtain arrangements – do not belong in this environment. Nor would I advise keeping traditional musical instruments such as a piano or a harp in a garden room as they suffer from the bright light and the humidity. However, it is a wonderful place to listen to music, and a sound system with pairs of small speakers at roof level is a good idea. Like any other room in the house, it is the details that bring a garden room to life.

Above The mauvish-grey conservatory exterior corresponds with the grey Buckinghamshire stone of the house, the grey-and-white woodwork, and grey-and-white planting. Inside, the furnishings are warmer, with honey-coloured tables and chairs, a china storage cupboard, and an assortment of coloured cushions.

Below The rough, woody interior style of beach huts and boat houses translates well to garden rooms. The boarding here has been stained chalky white, the starting point for a colour scheme of ecru and beige tones, combined with blue.

Colour and texture

With glass buildings, the interior and exterior colours are visible together, and this relationship should be exploited. The exterior elements of paving, paths and plants, as well as the external colours of the garden room, should be taken into consideration when planning the interior – the internal walls and framework, furniture and fabrics, the floors, blinds, and yet more plants.

Texture is, in many respects, the essence of garden room style, allowing rough outdoor elements to be incorporated into the interior in a manner that might be unsuitable to other rooms. Many garden rooms contain at least one solid wall, usually part of the external walls of the house, which can provide the starting point for the overall colour scheme. Garden rooms receive more daylight and sunshine, both direct and reflected, than other rooms, and this should be a consideration when choosing colours and finishes. White, for example, is the traditional colour of conservatories, but it can be harsh in sunlight, while brilliant contemporary colours sometimes appear garish.

Below *The minimal, glass construction of this conservatory depends on colour for its identity, with the bold use of yellow stucco inside extending out into the garden. Outside, the planting scheme is all the more effective for using only red or mauve flowers.*

Left *When I added a small lean-to conservatory to my London home, the idea was to provide a breakfast area and a link with the garden, which is densely planted with bold evergreens. I followed the green theme into the house with apple-green woodwork, green blinds and a green scagliola table. The scheme is especially successful in sunny weather.*

Top *Another interior using green, but this time combined with chalky-white match-boarding on the walls and incorporating highlights of bright lime green, all with an emphasis on texture.*

Above *The whites, ecru, buffs and brown of natural materials: a Siena stone floor, a bleached-willow lounger and footstool, traditional striped fabrics designed by Susan Hirsh, linen cushions and pots.*

This indoor pool has a very basic colour scheme, with an attractive rhythm of shadows produced by the bars of the timber-and-glass roof. The line of the rear wall is relieved by arches, including the central niche with potted palms.

Above A vibrant red, white
and green table setting, laid
for a special occasion with a
pretty Oriental-print cloth,
check cushion covers,
colourful plates and
napkins, and dramatic
flower arrangements. A wire
hanging basket complete
with candle holders hangs
from the ceiling.
Below Soft greens mixed
with cream, natural linen
and bleached wood. These
colours are effective with the
plant-greens outside and the
lime-green plants on the
table inside.

It is important to consider year-round use in the decorative scheme, as a colour that looks stunning in hot July sunshine may seem rather foolish on a damp February morning. There are, however, consistent themes in the garden room colour palette, the first being greens, the basic colour of plants. Green offers the widest variety, from lime green, to mid-greens to the deep viridian of moss, with the grey-green of lavender, beautiful purple-sage green and the blue-green of sea holly: any of these can be used as a starting point and combined with blues, yellows, whites and buffs, or even orange and purple. Another theme is earth colours – brick with ochre walls and terracotta pots, for example, or pale limestone floors with stone-coloured woodwork and stoneware pots. Generally, lighter tones are more successful for garden rooms. Some schemes have dark colours but, unless dark shades are used in small or specific ways, they can seem out of place in a garden room. No other room in the house has a stronger sense of season, so colours can be modified around the year to reflect this, with brilliant colours in the summer and warmer tones in autumn and winter.

Above A dining table, with a
top of scagliola made as a
beautiful, durable, imitation
of Siena marble. The chairs
have a bold stripe of woven
horse-hair fabric.

Above British fashion
designer Zandra Rhodes'
garden room, suffused with
pink light and decorated with
a trademark "Z" and zany
swans covered in pebbles in
front of Andrew Logan's
broken-mirrorwork.

Right I used traditional
coloured lime plaster on the
walls of this Chelsea Flower
Show conservatory to produce
a more subtle, deeper colour
than can be achieved with
emulsion paint. It was also a
perfect background for the
large kumquat trees in
terracotta pots, and the
natural oak table and chairs.
The table setting echoes the
colours of the trees with
orange and green plates,
green candle sticks and
glasses, and orange fruit.
The enormous decorative
wire chandelier was made
specially for the occasion.
The chairs outside are
galvanised so that they can be
left out year-round.

A seat constructed from two shaped wicker benches and specially-made cushions, fitted round a potted cinnamon tree. The octagonal seat corresponds with the form of the room. The conservatory is finished with sea green and silver blue paint, and the floor is white limestone.

Opposite *Comfortable rattan-cane chairs contribute to the inviting setting in a conservatory with a colour scheme of terracotta and deep bronze-green.*

Below *Wicker furniture for use outdoors is traditionally made with an open-weave pattern to reduce the weight, making it easier to carry. The furniture here has been painted the same colour as the old iron windows.*

Overleaf *A wicker chair based on a traditional Orkney pattern, designed to keep draughts out and the occupant warm. A lining of cotton prints has been added to this chair and the wing-chair next to it.*

Above and below People most commonly associate garden-room furniture with striped upholstery fabric. Shown here are two versions with green and white stripes – combined below with plain green side cushions and green painted wicker.
Opposite Wicker furniture from Marston & Langinger made from natural buff-coloured willow. The table has traditional barley-twist feet. The conservatory is two storeys, connected by a spiral staircase. Outside is a small courtyard decorated with trellis and potted shrubs, including mimosa and camellias.

Wicker is made from various plants – rattan cane from Asia, particularly the Philippines, and a number of species of willow native to Europe. Willow is grown either as small plants cut annually, or as trees grown along the banks of streams and rivers, cut back at the end of each winter to produce a crop of short shoots, which is harvested at the end of the following season. These shoots, called withyes, are woven together while damp and pliant, with or without the bark, to make anything from baskets to chairs, tables and sofas, and the material is left in its natural buff colour, or it can be bleached or painted. Wicker furniture has the charm of instrinsic simplicity – it is entirely handmade (and environmentally sound) and is lightweight and strong. It is best used indoors, or outdoors on a veranda, but painted wicker can occasionally be left on an open terrace.

Painting wicker can remove any rustic, home-spun associations, and treated this way, it can be used effectively in an urban setting, particularly if the colours are subtle and matt-finished and combine well with fabrics and surrounding shades.

Left Metal furniture designs look completely at home in the garden room. This gracefully curved, traditional wrought-iron table with a black slate top was designed by Josephine Marston.

Below Mosaic is an attractive, venerable-looking material for table tops. It is time-consuming to make, involving the cutting and fitting of thousands of tiny pieces of stone or glass. Much of the appeal comes from the minute variation in colour and texture of the individual pieces, or tesserae. Mosaic tables normally have an iron base, and although they can be used out of doors, they are generally not weatherproof. A simpler, less expensive form of mosaic, zellig, is made in North Africa from small pieces of coloured, glazed ceramic.

Tables and chairs A large table will almost certainly be needed, especially if the garden room is used for informal dining. A round or oval table is often the most suitable, but the shape and size of the room and other furnishing requirements ultimately dictate the shape of the table. Straightforward natural materials are best, in finishes that are easy to maintain and which continue to look good as they become worn. Tops made out of stone – slate, sandstone, limestone, unpolished marble – work well, although they tend to be heavy, making the table difficult to move, especially if it is large. Glass, either frosted or clear, and steel, such as old French cafe tables, are lighter and more versatile. Wicker and rattan can be used, but need to have a level surface to be practical.

Ceramic tiles and mosaic-work give the greatest scope for colour, texture and artistry. Unpolished wood is also suitable, particularly hard, grainy timbers such as oak, elm and teak, which develop a weathered appearance. There are also some unusual finishes: scagliola made from coloured plaster and stone in imitation of marble; copper- or zinc-covered wood, and prettily coloured glazed ceramic tops.

__Above__ Polished steel high-backed chair in a classically simple design.
__Below left__ Wire chair with a soft cushion for added comfort, covered in sage-green-and-white cotton print.
__Below right__ A pretty wrought-iron chair, based on a turn-of-the-century French design, with a plaited, springy steel seat.

Left A Gothic-pattern, wire dining chair. Wirework is surprisingly strong and lightweight, and can be prettily painted, but always needs a cushion.
Below Unusual iron chairs made with sheet steel cut to make a graceful back, and with perforated steel seats. The arms terminate in brass swans' heads.

Opposite A beautiful wrought-iron table base with a black fossil-stone top. The chairs in the foreground are based on a traditional French pattern, while at the back, next to the door, is a chair I designed in stiff wire.

Above *A simple iron breakfast table with a sandstone top. In the background is a pair of hardy chusan palms which, in a reasonably warm environment, will grow into trees.*

Below *A four-seater wire bench based on a Regency design. Conceived for use outside, it is lightweight and practical for use indoors with the addition of cushions.*

Side and console tables are both functional and attractive as part of the furniture arrangement in a garden room. Small coffee tables of metal and glass, and larger, more robust tables that can double up as seating are also useful.

Chairs for use at the table generally fall between garden and dining chairs in style and are usually made of metal – cast-iron, aluminium and steel – either painted or polished or with a rust finish. Wirework chairs are strong and light and, if galvanised, can also be used in the garden. Wicker chairs are mostly too bulky for use at the table, but combined with iron or wood, or made by Lloyd Loom, they are much more successful for this purpose. Metal and wicker chairs invariably require seat cushions. Most of these materials can be painted to co-ordinate with tables and other furniture in the room. Garden rooms are good showrooms for quirky occasional chairs – antique wickerwork, for example, which may be too delicate for everyday use.

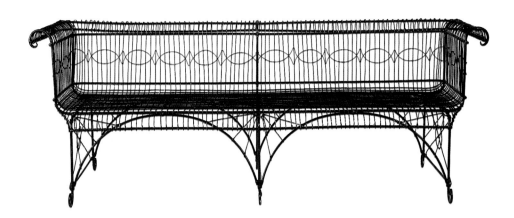

Opposite In the Regency period, chairs and benches were popularly made from strips of steel, rolled into a reeded section, wrought and riveted together. This reproduction chair is next to a new, round iron dining table, with a slate top that matches the decorative slate strips in the floor.

Above Garden furniture made out of teak or iroko can be brightened with cloth and colourful china (these plates are antique Wedgwood with a leaf pattern). The terrace here is convenient to the kitchen, which is reached through the conservatory. On the left, not visible, is a brick-built barbecue.

Right *Night lights are an easy, inexpensive form of lighting but are most effective in multitude. Here is an assortment of green and clear hanging-glass holders, suspended from a wire hanging basket.*

Below *Just as in a drawing room, standard lamps are especially useful in corners or behind furniture. This straightforward telescopic bronze design compliments metal garden room furniture.*

Lighting

The lighting of a glass-covered room, flooded with natural daylight, presents a specific problem. Where there is glass, light will be lost out into the garden or sky rather than reflected back as soft background light, as in other rooms. Consequently, a number of low-intensity lamps is better than a few bright ones. Although the style may be different, the same type of electric lamp can be used in the garden room as would be used elsewhere in the house – table and standard lamps, wall brackets, hanging lamps and low-voltage starlights set high in the roof.

Most appealing of all are candles, or oil lamps. Tiny night lights in coloured pressed-glass holders make delightful occasional lighting. In summer, when the doors and windows are open, candles are generally best in clear-glass hurricane shades, which are available in a variety of sizes, including impressively large ones. Inexpensive oil lamps create a surprisingly bright light and can be long-burning. Small low-voltage downlighters set in the roof, or starlights (if the roof is constructed of wood) provide straightforward background lighting and are especially effective in conjunction with a dimmer switch.

Above A Portuguese candelabra assembled from numerous turned-wood spindles illuminates the table, while sidelights provide background lighting.

Right Simple garden room table or side lights.

Above left *An old oil lamp with reflector, bought in southern Spain, makes ideal lighting fixed to a window frame.*
Below *Plain hurricane lamps on brass brackets are a simple, attractive lighting option fixed around the sides of a wooden building.*

Right *A traditional, Moorish lantern from Fez in Morocco, with intricately pierced patterns and clear and coloured glass. Modern reproductions are rarely as well made.*

Left A candle holder with a shade, made entirely of bamboo in Bali.
***Below right** A hanging electric lamp, based on a Turkish kiosk design, looks perfect in a conservatory roof.*

Hanging lamps and chandeliers are particularly suited to garden rooms, and are opportunities for striking decorative features – suspended from the roof over a dining table, for example. If these lamps or chandeliers are designed for candles, a rise-and-fall arrangement, like those for hanging baskets, can easily be rigged up.

In a new building, a lighting circuit with sockets for individual side and table lights can be installed so that they can be controlled by a single switch. The electrical plan should include outside lights – a consideration which not only contributes indirectly to the overall lighting within the room, but is also useful for evenings on the terrace, when a good daytime view can be illuminated artificially and enjoyed equally at night. Special waterproof lamps must be used outside, however, and these can be fitted into the framework or adjacent masonry, providing the doors of the garden room do not fold over them. Simple traditional designs from brass, bronze, nickel or painted metal, and glass designs based on old porch or hallway styles work well for this purpose. As this type of lamp is generally not shaded, low-wattage clear bulbs give the best effect.

83   DECORATIVE ELEMENTS

Left *The fireplace was an important feature in the plans for this conservatory, and it can be used for either coal or wood. At night the light from a wood fire, combined with candles and small star-lights in the roof, makes the perfect setting for a meal.*

Above *Hurricane lamps are ideal for large slow-burning candles, and can be used indoors as part of the table setting, or outdoors on a terrace or in the garden.*
Below *A French candelabra in bronze, with banana and palm leaves, and a tiny serpent writhing upwards.*

Above *Soft furnishings mark the transition from the hard surfaces of the garden room to the cozy warmth of the drawing room.*
Below *Two cotton prints: Trailing ivy by Susan Hirsh of Marston & Langinger, and Brunswick by Johanna Woods.*
Opposite *Bright colours used in the garden room: a brilliant silk stripe with a Paisley-type throw over a Lloyd Loom chair. Bright fabrics work best in association with strongly coloured flowers, but check – they can fade.*

Fabrics and soft furnishings

As with many other aspects of the garden room, fabrics and soft furnishings offer an opportunity to create a style quite different from the rest of the house. Striped fabrics are traditionally associated with garden rooms, and they look particularly good in this setting. Options for using stripes vary from the familiar mix of striped cushions off-setting floral scatter cushions or a combination of different striped fabrics, to a contemporary look of bold stripes in natural tones, contrasted with cushions covered in ethnic fabrics. Floral print cushions always look right in garden rooms amongst the growing plants and flowers, while coarse canvas and linens come into their own in this area of natural textures and materials. Small cushions covered in tribal fabrics, appliqué, needlepoint or even simple embroidery also work well here.

Reversing the old rule that the cloth should be removed from the table for dinner, it softens a garden room to use a tablecloth for evening, and also in winter. Antique French fabric (perhaps quilted), an African print or chenille are possibilities.

Overleaf *A table illuminated by diffused sunlight shining through natural flax blinds printed with a lime-green stripe. The coarse linen cloth sets off the table of old planks laid with linen and cream china. This conservatory demonstrates a highly effective mix of soft greens, beiges and cream with highlights of lime green.*

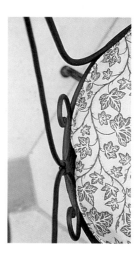

DECORATIVE ELEMENTS

Opposite A pleasing scheme of violet-and-buff striped blinds, plain cotton cushion and check scatter cushions.
Overleaf The brilliant colours of the cushions, built-in sofa, rug and hanging fabrics, transform an otherwise plain garden room.
Below The simplicity of stripes is especially successful in the garden room. The small armless sofa used here is covered in an antique-style, Pinchbeck, woven cotton stripe.

Above The traditional choice for blinds in a glass roof is pinoleum, woven reeds of fine pine, left natural or painted.

In winter, rugs can be put down on the hard floors to create a sense of warmth. Simple, natural textures such as abaca (banana fibre), sea grass, jute or even woven, twisted paper rugs suit a garden room. Dhurries also look good on stone, and the traditional earthy colours of kilims blend well with terracotta flooring.

Curtains, though not appropriate to garden rooms, may be needed for privacy, while blinds over windows and loose voile or muslin drapes create a beautiful soft light. The fabrics in a garden room should be comfortable, with relaxed sofas, perhaps with loose covers that can be changed seasonally, and plainly finished, not over-stuffed cushions with self-piping and modest fringes.

Consideration should be given to the bright light that penetrates a garden room and can fade fabrics. Even specialist fabrics are not entirely resistant to sunlight, and the only certain way to protect expensive fabrics is to keep the blinds down in mid-summer. That said, the textiles used in a garden room should not be too precious and should also adapt easily for use on the terrace and lawn.

Gossamer-thin cotton blinds,
suspended on charming hooks
fixed to the framework of the
windows, diffuse the light
and provide a degree of
privacy while retaining an
awareness of the garden
outside.

95

5

Architectural elements

Garden rooms, more than any other in the house, depend on the structural elements for their decorative effect. They are rooms without fitted carpets, wallpaper and, usually without curtains. But they will have fine big windows and doors, a bold roof, particularly if it is glass, and possibly panelling and a cornice, elements which should be scaled to each other and unified by the colour scheme. Beginning with the floor, the room could have underfloor heating with cast-iron grilles around the perimeter, a stone or wood skirting and panelling up to window-sill height, either framed mouldings, possibly containing radiators, or much simpler match-boarding (there is some illustrated full-height on page 107). The windows and doors can be attractively moulded with decorative glazing bars that create a pattern around the room. Similarly, the frame of the building may be plain, moulded or, in a large structure such a poolhouse, finished with pilasters or free-standing columns of iron or turned wood. A cornice carried around the room can provide a unifying element.

Glass The nineteenth century saw the advent of cheap sheet glass, but it was another hundred years before the introduction of safety glass, which is treated to break into small blunt pieces, and laminated glass, which is a sandwich of tough plastic holding the glass together. Further developments in glass include sealed-unit double-glazing, which dramatically reduces condensation and noise and makes a room much warmer, and the invention of low-emissivity glass with its virtually invisible coating that reflects heat back into the room, making double-glazing as efficient as triple glazing in terms of insulation.

Although the great improvements in glass technology are recent, the techniques of glass decoration were refined in medieval times, and include leaded lights in decorative patterns. Made from clear, textured, coloured or patterned glass and assembled with lead or brass framing, these are used as friezes in fan-lights for doors, or as decorative features in triangular gables. Frosted glass, either sandblasted or etched with a lacy pattern, is useful for privacy and for obscuring an unattractive view without loss of light.

Above *Burgundy limestone flooring, laid in random slabs with skirtings of the same material, in a conservatory and glazed corridor. The fireplace, in a West of England stone, and the textured stucco walls relate closely to the grain of the floor.*
Below *Herringbone-pattern brick paving compliments the texture of the brick, stone and oak of a traditional conservatory.*
Opposite *The floor, a combination of old flagstone and cobbles, has an attractive texture leading through the beds of glasshouse plants.*

Floors The style of a garden room is derived from the combination of architectural features, but in particular the floor – stone, terracotta, brick, or possibly wood – which should be selected for its natural texture and colour. The first consideration is whether the floor should be a continuation of a connecting room, the kitchen for example, with the same flooring material running through both, or a break with the adjoining rooms, with a change in style and materials, perhaps further emphasized by a change in level. If the intention is to fold the doors back in summer to create one large area incorporating the terrace, then a frost-resistant flooring material such as sandstone, certain limestones or ceramic paving can be used inside and out.

Durable materials that will remain unaffected by sunlight, variations of temperature or moisture are best. For this reason, wool carpets are unsuitable. Varieties of limestone range from smooth creamy-white, through biscuit-textured Siena limestone to hard pinkish-brown Burgundy limestone. Marble offers diverse patterns and colours, including cream-coloured antique-looking forms of travertine.

Top left to bottom right
*Old Yorkstone flags,
Burgundy stone, white
limestone with brown
travertine insets, Siena
limestone, terracotta with
white stone insets, rustic
terracotta with a kilim rug.*

Right *Reclaimed Cambridge
bricks were chosen here to
reinforce a sense of the garden
outdoors, with their rough
surface and earth-colour.*

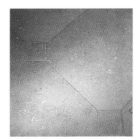

Left A typical Victorian ceramic floor in a Gothic-revival geometric pattern with decorated encaustic tiles around the perimeter and inset amongst the plain tiles.

Handmade terracotta tiles, with their natural texture due to the mixing of clays and variations in firing, can be both beautiful and simple. Generally, pinkish-buff rather than deep red forms of terracotta are easier to incorporate into a decorative scheme. Nothing beats brick, usually secondhand pavoirs, for rustic appeal. The most familiar form of sandstone is Yorkstone, which is non-slip and can be used inside and out. Old worn Yorkstone flags as large as 120cm (4 feet) are standard for terraces. These can also be used inside, but can be hard on furniture legs. For continuity between interior and exterior, new smooth-sawn Yorkstone can be laid inside, with old flags outside. Certain stone floors, especially combined with a cool colour scheme, can appear hard and cold on grey winter days. The effect can be softened by laying a rug or matting over them, which can be kept down throughout the year or removed in the summer. Wood flooring is also a possibility; oak and elm are both good for this purpose, but dryness and moisture tend to cause cracks between the boards. Finally, sea grass, coir or sisal matting are inexpensive alternatives, though they may wear out sooner.

Top right to bottom left Tuscany sandstone with a striped cotton rug; antique marble with a coloured sisal rug; pale limestone with a garden-theme rug; oak-framed floor with panels of terracotta, and a rug woven from natural sea grass and stencilled in the pattern of trellis, leaves and berries.

A new conservatory designed to look old with distressed paint finishes and "crumbling" plasterwork. The neutral floor is contemporary and does not distract from the faux ageing effect.

Above A roughly finished
painted wall, decorated with
a collection of sun-motif disks
ranging in size from a coat
button to a dinner plate.
Climbers hang down from
the roof.
Below Ordinary trellis
painted pale blue against a
cream background makes an
attractive colour
combination with passion
flowers, which quickly can be
trained over walls.

Walls

Solid walls should be robust-looking with a natural clear-sealed finish of old stone or brick, providing there are no modern alterations as, for example, when a new doorway has been created. They can also be painted with a cement-based masonry paint or traditional lime paint, which has a beautiful deep colour. Plastered walls are best simply cement-rendered, leaving the natural texture of mortar to be covered with a coat of paint. Applying several coats as thin washes in slightly different tones gives a subtle finish. Alternatively, in a room with wooden doors and lots of wood-framed windows, the walls can be wood-boarded as a way of harmonizing the glazed and solid areas, for a style suggestive of boat houses and sport pavilions, especially when painted in drab or lime-white shades.

Walls can easily be decorated with a pattern of contrasting shells, cockles, mussels, clams or more exotic abalones, or murex mixed with ordinary pebbles of flint and even coal. To make friezes, panels, and more ambitious shell pictures, the usual method is to press them into wet mortar, one section at a time, or glue them to the unpainted wall.

Whatever the finish, it should be a surface that can take nails and other fixtures such as trellises. These usually need to be specially made, and more finely constructed than

those used outside, in a diamond pattern or with arches or circles, perhaps forming a frieze around openings and beneath the roof. A good alternative is metal trellis (see overleaf).

Right As an alternative to
plaster, this conservatory was
boarded with wide beaded
pine and finished with matt
lime-white paint.

GARDEN ROOM STYLE

Opposite Wire trellis offers
an easy and attractive way of
decorating garden room
walls, and is excellent for
training plants; here, the
tender passiflora, Princess
Eugenie, climbs across the
room.

Above Walls decorated by an
abundance of climbers and
potted plants, and trellis.
The opposite wall is reflected
in a mirror.

Heating, cooling and shading

The heating of a garden room should be efficient enough to provide comfortable temperatures, even in a conservatory on a snowy winter day. A new building will have insulation within the floors and walls, either sufficiently-thick timber framing or insulated metal, double-glazing with low-emissivity glass, and draught-proofing seals around the windows and doors.

The existing central heating is usually extended into the new room. Radiators are largely regarded as a necessary evil, but high-quality pressed-steel radiators and cast-iron designs can be attractive. Cast-iron grilles set into the floor, with radiator pipes fitted beneath, are stylish and perfect in conservatories, reducing cold draughts and the risk of condensation. Another underfloor heating system, using a small bore pipe snaked back and forth over the insulation within the thickness of the floor, is unobtrusive but reacts slowly to changes of temperature or new settings. Electric underfloor heating is generally insufficiently powerful.

Above Fans help to cool in summer. If there are vents at the top of the roof, have the fans set to draw air up and out. Plain cast-iron fans like this example, specially constructed for conservatory roofs, are best.

Below Traditional cast-iron grilles, with central heating beneath, are an effective, stylish way of heating garden rooms. Fitted around the perimeter of a conservatory, they keep the windows and doors warm and reduce the likelihood of condensation.

Opposite This formal French fire surround in a rich brown marble would more usually be associated with a reception room, but with a simple grate it is successful amongst plants in a garden room.

Additional heating can be provided by an open fire, which is always dramatic, particularly with January frosts outside. Open heating can be connected to the boiler, allowing the conservatory to be kept warm regardless of whether the central heating is on in the remainder of the house – this is an important consideration for conservatory plants. While it is relatively simple to design a glass building that will be warm in winter, it will not be easy to keep it cool in summer unless certain elements are incorporated into the design. Ventilation is the first requirement: about a third of the windows should open, and in warm weather it should be possible to fold the doors right back. Roof ventilation is essential, and is normally electric; a special control, which will also operate the heating with a thermostat, should be used to avoid having the heat on while the ventilators are open. Anti-sun glass may be used to reduce the greenhouse effect of glass, which naturally converts light to heat. A fan or fans can help, especially in a south-facing building. Blinds are highly effective on a glass roof, both to cool the room and to reduce the glare from direct sun. In a hot or humid climate, air conditioning is normal but this prevents the enjoyment of open windows and doors.

Above This conservatory, which I built at the Castello di San Polo in Chianti, has doors which fold right back to cope with the heat of Tuscan summers. While a conservatory should be double-glazed and draught-proof in winter, it is important to be able to open lots of windows and doors in the summer. Ridge ventilators in the roof are equally essential.

Opposite Opening and closing conservatory doors is the most basic of ventilation devices.

6

Accessories All those small items – a hazel trug with garden twine, copper plant labels and an old trowel, prettily painted wirework jardinières, old watering cans, brass hand-sprayers, buckets, and stacks of old mossy flowerpots – are quite irresistibly attractive with their colour and texture, and their combination of clutter and formality. The main materials for this type of object are wirework, ranging from small pot holders to large plant stands and even benches; terracotta, whether functional horticultural pots or decorative designs with basketwork patterns and rope handles; basketwork, which can include expensive craftsman-made examples of great beauty; wooden items such as trays, including split-chestnut baskets; galvanised ironwork, copperwork and brasswork. These items, some decorative, most very practical, offer points of interest in the garden room, especially if they are old. Small antique shops and country markets are a regular source of pots, gardening tools and watering cans, and wire jardinières.

Plants and planting

As a child I used to visit a glasshouse near home which was always warm – a quiet, moist world with a grapevine spread across the roof, a jasmine with clouds of white, scented blossoms in February, benches covered in pots of geraniums, and beneath, amongst the pipes, dozens of tiny ferns. It had a special greenhouse smell (probably part chemical) that I loved, and those visits contributed to my interest in conservatories and garden rooms in general. Of course, not everybody wants a jungle, but a garden room would not be complete without some plants. What to grow depends partly on the room – how big it is, what direction it faces and how much sun it receives, how it is heated, and what ventilation and shading is available. How the room is used – as an essential place for meals or as an occasional room – and how it is furnished and in what style, should also be taken into account. The plants will be of three types: climbers, restricted to an area of trellis or allowed to climb over the walls and across the roof; hanging baskets; and plants in tubs and pots, either single or massed together in groups.

__Opposite__ A collection of evergreen glasshouse plants in a newly built conservatory which, though suited to people, is given over to plants. __Top to bottom__ White primulas, growing in a shallow, patinaed terracotta pot with puzzle rings; and delicately woven, white-painted wire baskets.

A tall octagonal-plan glasshouse, big enough for a huge palm, bananas, a mimosa, and other large, tender plants. Here, everything is grown in decorative terracotta pots, with attractive under-planting.

Above An antique teak chest, probably Indian, with a hand-made grille of wrought iron, used as a tub for an array of plants.
Below left A long-tom pot, with variegated ivy grown up a pyramidal wire frame.
Below right The simplicity of finely-coloured hand-thrown clay raises the flower pot from greenhouse to garden room.

A large room can contain several planting arrangements, with the concentration of plants increasing gradually from the house towards the garden. As a general rule, a sunny conservatory will be better for blossoms, particularly Mediterranean plants, such as bougainvillea, plumbago and oleander, while plants selected for their leaves and leaf patterns, such as palms and ferns, suit a shady room. The majority of garden rooms are well heated, usually by central heating, but unless the heat is kept on at night, or there is a separate arrangement of pipework and controls for the garden room, many plants will suffer at night. Plants can also suffer from too much sun and inadequate ventilation – conditions that can be controlled by blinds and, in new buildings, adequate roof ventilation as well as plenty of windows and doors that open. A further consideration is humidity. Many plants are sold with instructions for regular spraying, something which, in practice, simply does not happen. But plants grouped together can create their own moist microclimate in the room, or plants that thrive in low humidity can be chosen.

Top *Paper-white narcissi growing up through wheat seed planted in a simple terracotta pan.*
Above *A fine, beautifully coloured wicker basket planted with pinkish-white hippiastrums, supported with a frame of dogwood, and under-planted to cover the bulbs.*
Far right *A grey-green, glaucous succulent growing in a cork pot.*
Below *A selection of English hand-made terracotta pots and wicker baskets.*

This conservatory houses a jungle of plants that look attractive against the green interior. The blinds, made by Marston & Langinger, match the colour of the woodwork. The windows have Gothic arches to increase the architectural impact of the building in the surrounding grounds.

Above *An old terracotta pot with the glaze wearing off perfectly matches the planting in autumn.*
Below *An attractive lead tub fashioned by garden designer Anthea Gibson.*

Right *An antique pedestal supports a potted plant container. Here, new and old, bright and faded colours, are successfully combined.*

Above *A Gothic wardian case. These were popular on window sills, or even built into the windows of Victorian houses, separating the drawing room from the street with a miniature world of ferns and mosses. Behind the case is a curious iron cake-stand plant-holder, and farther back, a sculpted shepherd rests, leaning on his crook.*

Left *Decorative and practical, a moveable plant stand incorporating a metal tray for gravel.*

Above *Plants growing on every surface soften the profile of this conservatory.*

It is ideal to be able to rearrange the furniture and plants seasonally or for special occasions, and to move developing plants around to the best advantage. Climbers, however, which provide interest on a higher level, and include many exciting conservatory plants – jasmines, passion flowers, stephanotis, hoyas and plumbagos – must be in a fixed position in a substantial container such as a large pot or tub, or a planter. Earth beds are not really suitable for private houses as they are inflexible and difficult to maintain. A clutter of small pots, especially house plants on window sills, should also be avoided; it is much better to have a few dramatic well-shaped specimens in large, well-made pots. Useful examples are cycads which, though evergreen, throw up shuttlecocks of fresh leaves regularly; citrus fruit – a Meyer lemon, or calamondin orange which produces lots of small oranges and scented blossoms; and mimosa (*acacia dealbata*) with feathery, grey-green leaves and clouds of yellow spring blossoms. On a smaller scale, bulbs offer seasonal variety and can be grown in interesting ways: catalogues offer many exotic specimens and varieties. To grow plants successfully, the single most important factor is watering, which means seasonal adjustment of quantity, and care not to over or under water. At some point, plants grown behind glass will inevitably suffer infestations: red spider mite, white fly, aphids (green fly), and scale insects are most common. The only practical treatment is to take the plants outside and spray them thoroughly with a suitable insecticide or natural remedy, and to repeat this two or three times so that any eggs are also killed. For a perfect collection of plants at all times, the ideal solution is a small separate greenhouse.

Above Spanish moss growing in a wire basket, hanging from the roof of a conservatory, compliments the grey colour scheme of the building. *Below* To be successful, hanging baskets need lots of light, and should be planted with specimens which will naturally cover the underside.

Opposite *A smart garden room with a polished marble floor and iron furniture, including a useful tripod stand in a design derived from a traditional pot-stand. To the right is a large iron wedding-cake stand, a decorative and practical way of growing and displaying a variety of plants in an attractive group in the room.*

Above left *Plant containers can be made of the most unlikely material (to make them waterproof, line them with pieces of folded plastic), such as broken china, shells, bark, wicker and fir cones. The cyclamens in small pots are growing up through a covering of moss.*

Above right *Wire baskets, reproductions of Victorian originals.*

Left *Jardinières are useful for putting together groups of plants (which grow better with the increased humidity). A dozen plants of the same type can make an instant bold display of colour.*

Below *An amusing figurative plant pot with a perfect wig of greenery spilling out.*

Top and bottom The simplicity of clear and hand-blown glass is perfect for cut flowers in the garden room. Here are yellow raunculas above, and tulips above and below.

Accessories The cultivation of plants is an important function of the room, and specially constructed staging and shelves may be designed for this purpose. Metal or wood, perhaps teak or oak, can be used for legs, with slatted wood or metal on top. Staging, which should be at a convenient working height, is particularly effective with gravel-filled trays to catch the excess water that provides a humid environment for the plants. Shelves on shaped wooden or cast-iron brackets can be fitted to the window frames, and they look neatest aligned with horizontal glazing bars. In a large conservatory, the centre can feature a rectangular or circular tiered staging, which is particularly handsome with a tree growing up through the centre. Ferns can be grown in the damp atmosphere of a romantic grotto built against a wall and suitably waterproofed with blocks of tufa stone (from garden centres), but they will need supervision to ensure that moisture and humidity are adequate.

Opposite It is the eclectic collection of objects that lend the scene its garden room style: a wrought-iron table with inset terracotta top; a pressed and framed gunnera leaf; the bamboo-shaded candle sticks; the woven wire holder for the succulent plant on the table; a rush basket containing the hibiscus bush; the patinated terracotta finials.

Left An Indian swing fits well in the height of a conservatory and makes a fine feature in the room.

Below A painted wooden storage container prettily decorated in a Persian style, with a hinged lid that serves as a table.

A garden room atmosphere can be extended to any room which offers adequate lighting for plants. Be creative with the placement and choice of containers and you will be rewarded with pleasing results. A garden room is also the ideal setting to display a collection. Plates, jugs and glass are completely at home in a room flooded with natural light and can be prettily displayed on painted wood shelves, glass-enclosed cabinets or wirework stands.

Opposite The wall of this conservatory is decorated with "cut-out" Chinese urns over a console table of potted, scented white roses. The chairs are by Beaumont & Fletcher.
Above A galvanised wire rack, which can be used for plates, cups and saucers, small pots and ornaments.
Below A nineteenth-century print of a glasshouse in a trellis-pattern frame – ideal for a conservatory.

Above Jugs are generally easier than watering cans for watering potted plants. This example is crocodile-embossed brass.

Below Agate-pattern tom-thumb flower pots made by skillfully blending three colours of clay.

Right A nineteenth-century baker's rack used for a display of pots, watering equipment, plants and candle sticks. At bottom right are carved and turned wooden finials, which are used on the apexes of glass roofs.

Above *A tap-and-sink fountain – an attractive and practical cast-iron design with room for a bucket or watering can beneath the tap. The sink, covered in a grating, can be set into the floor.*
Below *Kibble Palace. The humid atmosphere of the pool beneath a Victorian dome is a perfect environment for the royal fern, osmundis regalis, which has grown into an enormous bush around the tree-fern.*

Fountains and statues

The sound of trickling water always contributes to a mood of repose and a sense of contact with nature. Fountain heads built into or against a wall are usually in the form of heads – human, lion or dolphin – with water streaming from pouting lips to splash into a pool beneath. Together these make an attractive feature which can be combined with moisture-loving ferns, papyrus and arum lilies. Installation is not simple, requiring completely waterproof construction and an electric pump. Alternatively, a glazed ceramic or cast-iron wall fountain connected to the water supply from the house is a decorative and practical tap-and-sink arrangement for the conservatory. In a larger room, it is possible to have a detached pool and fountain in traditional tiered marble surmounted by a cherub, or to design a modern water feature using water effects: pellicules, jet and foam. Statues, although currently rather out of fashion, are particularly associated with Georgian orangeries, and usually take the classical forms of Flora, Pan and shepherdesses, and Victorian alabaster statues.

Opposite *A pool built against the inside of an orangery, with spouts in the form of Haddonstone grotesques.*

Left *The lush interior of the grand conservatory at Flintham Hall has a central pool with a finely carved stone Italian fountain, which makes an attractive splashing sound. It also helps keep the atmosphere moist for the delicate plants that are grown in the building.*

Below *Finely carved white Carrara statuary was popular in Victorian winter gardens. Good examples now fetch high prices at auctions.*

7

Using the garden room

Garden rooms generally incorporate two functioning areas; one that offers comfortable seating as a place to relax, and another with a table for meals and entertaining, or as a place to work. Garden rooms are a natural choice for any task that requires good light, and for children's activities. They are also very good for parties. In the right location, usually close to the kitchen, they are popular spaces that are regularly rearranged to suit a particular function. The doors, closed all winter, perhaps with a table in front of them, will be folded back onto the terrace in the summer and the furniture re-positioned accordingly. In the autumn, plants are brought in for the winter, while in the spring the garden room might be filled with narcissi and other bulbs. I often use the garden room for meals (especially breakfast and supper), for reading, socializing, and for working at home. This book was written in a garden room.

Entertaining and special occasions

For most of us, garden rooms are linked with eating and entertaining. On a sunny weekend morning the windows can be opened, and a table arranged with flowers and set specially for breakfast, rather than the hurried weekday routine of toast and coffee in the kitchen. In the evening, a table set with lots of candles or small lamps, pretty china, crystal and flowers makes a romantic and informal setting for supper instead of the stuffiness of a conventional dining room.

A garden room can also be used rather like a marquee and set up with tables of drinks and food for a garden party in the summer, particularly if there are large doors which can be hooked back. Barbecues on the terrace become a possibility even on windy or chilly evenings with the shelter of a garden room to eat in. A grill can be built inside, but will require a flue, and probably a fan for a forced draught, to be certain of success.

At Christmas and other holidays, a glass room will generally accommodate a tall tree or large-scale decorations, and can be accented with fairy lights, candles, night-lights, and glass ornaments, which will look magical inside and out.

Above A lively printed cloth and cheerful colours sidestep formality in this large conservatory. The planting and views of the garden make it a perfect location for entertaining.
Below Garden room plates: left, Spode with gardening motifs, and right, a practical pewter plate.
Overleaf A Marston & Langinger conservatory with a ceramic table beautifully set for afternoon tea. The glass jars on the widow sill offer a choice of flower teas. The flowers, delicate geraniums, astrantia and lady's mantle, are the perfect accessories for the food.

Opposite Space cleared in a greenhouse for lunch on a grey day in early summer. Behind the table are oleander, datura, a fuchsia, and other plants in flower. Green paint, and Gothic arches applied to the windows, prettify an otherwise plain glasshouse. In the foreground is a pressed steel chair in an unusual mid-century design.

Above *A table close to the folded-back doors enables the garden to be appreciated during the summer season, even if there is a chilly breeze.*

Opposite *A strong sense of occasion can be created by pushing back the potted palms, throwing a linen cloth over the table, and setting it for a formal meal.*

Opposite *Christmas in a conservatory, with a table cloth decorated with gold stars and applied lacework. Behind the enormous silver candlestick in the centre, the tree is decorated with old-fashioned candles.*

Right *I designed this pretty Gothic-decorated, two-storey conservatory at the back of the house in a London square. The owners wanted to bring more light into the house and create two new areas for eating and entertaining. At the bottom, the kitchen extends into an informal dining room with doors and steps leading to a courtyard garden. Above, the drawing room extends into a conservatory with a balcony, overlooking the garden and a small round table.*

Overleaf *Traditional conservatories provide lots of scope for Christmas decoration. They are high enough for a big tree, lights can be pinned around the framework, and night lights in coloured glass holders can be suspended from the roof. Outside is a reindeer made from wire with moss and ivy.*

LISTINGS

Conservatory Builders

OAK LEAF CONSERVATORIES LTD.
876 Davis Drive, Atlanta, GA 30327. Tel. 1.800.360.6283
Painted hardwood conservatories.

HERITAGE GARDEN HOUSE
City Visions Inc., 311 Seymour Street, Lansing, MI 48933. Tel. 517.372.3385
Classical, Victorian, 18th- and 20th-century conservatory kits.

FOUR SEASONS SUNROOMS
5005 Veterans Highway, Holbrook, NY 11741. Tel. 1.800.368.7732
Fully installed, competatively priced conservatories.

HARTFORD CONSERVATORIES
Call for local dealers. Tel. 1.800.963.8700
Website: http://www.hartford-con.com
Victorian, classical, and contemporary hardwood conservatories.

AMDEGA AND MACHIN CONSERVATORIES
3515 Lakeshore Drive, St. Josephs, MI 49085. Tel. 1.800.922.0110
Elegant residential and commercial conservatories.

TANGELWOOD CONSERVATORIES
Call for more information. Tel. 1.800.229.2925
Custom-designed and installed conservatories.

CANTERBURY CONSERVATORY
136 West 64th Street, Holland, MI 49423. Tel. 616.394.0303
Manufacturer and importer of English conservatories. Conservatory accessories: furniture, flooring and sculpture, etc.

THE AMERICAN CONSERVATORY CO., INC.
1380 Wayne Avenue, Indiana, PA 15701. Tel. 1.888.822.2485
Custom-designed conservatories.

MARSTON & LANGINGER LTD.
Call for more information. Tel. +44 (0) 171.823.6829
Website: http://www.marston-and-langiner.com
Top-quality custom conservatories.

SUN ROOM CO.
Delaware Valley, North Wales, Pennsylvania, 19454. Tel. 215.699.3747
Sun rooms and conservatories, mid-range, traditional designs.

Blinds

#1 BLINDS INTERNATIONAL
6371-3 Arc Way, Fort Myers, FL 33912. Tel. 1.800.866.5371
Comprehensive window blind retailer.

CONRAD
Call for more information. Tel. 415.626.3303
Designer window treatments utilizing natural fibers and unique textures.

GILA
P.O. Box 5068, Martinsville, VA 24115. Tel. 1.800.528.4481
Website: http://www.gilafilms.com
Ultraviolet protective window films.

HUNTER DOUGLAS
Call for local dealers. Tel. 1.800.866.5371
Fabric shading, blinds and window treatments.

PHIFER WIRE PRODUCTS, INC.
P.O. Box 1700, Tuscaloosa, AL 35403-1700. Tel. 1.800.874.3007
Specialized blinds for patios and porches.

WINDOW MODES
Call for more information. Tel. 914.592.4545
Custom-fabricated solar shading available as roller shades or motorized as solar Romans and as vertical blinds.

Furniture

McGUIRE
GD5-98, 151 Vermont Street, San Francicso, CA 94103. Tel. 1.800.662.4847
Wood and fabric furniture for gardens and interiors.

STICKLEY
Stickley Drive, P.O. Box 480, Manlius, NY 13104-0480. Tel. 315.682.5500
Wood and fabric furniture for gardens and interiors.

McKINNON AND HARRIS INC.
P.O. Box 4885, Richmond, VA 23220-1109. Tel. 804.355.7022
Fine garden furniture.

FRENCH WYRES
P.O. Box 131655, Tyler, TX 75713. Tel. 903.597.8322
American-made wire garden furnishings.

GIATI DESIGNS, INC.
614 Santa Barbara Street, Santa Barbara, CA 93101. Tel. 805.965.6535
Teak furniture, market umbrellas, interior and exterior textiles exclusively designed by Mark Singer.

GEORGE SMITH
73 Spring Street, New York, NY 10012. Tel. 212.226.4747
Website: http://www.georgesmith.com
Handmade furniture, fabrics, wallpaper, and hand-colored leather.

HOLLY HUNT COLLECTION
Call for information and local dealers. Tel. 310.855.1313
Simple elegant furnishings.

BARLOW TYRIE
1263 Glen Avenue, Suite 230, Moorestown, NJ 08057. Tel. 609.273.7878
Website: http://www.teak.com
Teak furniture designed in the English garden tradition.

MARSTON & LANGINGER LTD.
Call for more information. Tel. +44 (0) 171.823.6829
Website: http://www.marston-and-langiner.com
Comprehensive range of garden room furniture and accessories, lighting, and plant containers.

CANTERBURY CONSERVATORY
136 West 64th Street, Holland, MI 49423. Tel. 616.394.0303
Manufacturer and importer of English conservatories. Conservatory accessories: furniture, flooring and sculpture, etc.

Statuary and ornaments

ELIZABETH SCHUMACHER'S GARDEN ACCENTS
4 Union Hill Road, West Conshohocken, PA 19428. Tel. 610.825.5525
Hand-crafted garden ornaments.

SILBERT & RICE
P.O. Box 365, Short Hills, NJ 07078. Tel. 973.467.8266
Website: http://www.seilbert-rice.com
Terra cotta planters designed by American designers and handmade in Italy.

KENNETH LYNCH & SONS
P.O. Box 488, Wilton, CT 06897. Tel. 203.762.8363
Website: http://www.klynchandsons.com
Sculpture and statuary, planters and urns, topiary, and sundials.

FLORENTINE CRAFTSMAN INC.
46-24 28th Street, Long Island, NY 11101. Tel. 718.937.7632
Website: http:/ /www.florentinecraftsmen.com
Garden ornaments, statuary, fountains, and furniture.

RISING SUN GARDENS
4451 Route 27, Princeton, NJ 08540. Tel. 609.924.2743
Granite and marble lanterns, bowls, urns, fountains, and other garden ornaments.

STONE FOREST
P.O. Box 2840, Santa Fe, NM 87504. Tel. 505.986.8883
Japanese tradition with a contemporary design. Fountains, lanterns, stone sinks, and spheres.

KANE
110B Tweed Street, Pawtucket, RI 02861. Tel. 401.723.8622
Sculpted and cast fountains and sculptures.

GARDEN REGALIA
P.O. Box 721, Lakeville, CT 06039. Tel. 860.435.2210
Steel garden ornaments.

TOSCANO
17 E. Campbell Street, Arlington Heights, IL 60005. Tel. 847.255.6760
Re-creating 19th-century historical casts of classical figures, gargoyles, cherubs, and fountains.

TAKASHIMAYA
693 Fifth Avenue, New York, NY 10022. Tel. 212.350.0100
Garden room antiques as well as stylish new pots and accessories.

Glasshouses open to the public

BROOKLYN BOTANICAL GARDENS
100 Washington Avenue, Brooklyn, NY 11225. Tel. 718.622.4433
Steinhardt Conservatory.

CHICAGO BOTANICAL GARDENS
1000 Lake Cook Road, Glencoe, IL 60022. Tel. 847.835.5440
Educational greenhouses with a wet tropical rainforest, hot desert sands, and a warm temperate collection.

THE CLIMATRON - MISSOURI BOTANICAL GARDENS
4344 Shaw Boulevard, St. Louis, MO. Tel. 314.577.9441
Geodesic dome conservatory houses a tropical rainforest display.

COMO PARK CONSERVATORY
1325 Aida Place, St. Paul, MN 55103. Tel. 612.489.1740
Glass- and aluminum-Victorian building.

KROHN CONSERVATORY
Eden Park Drive, Cincinnati, OH 45202. Tel. 513.421.4086
The conservatory was rebuilt in 1933, and it boasts a 20-foot waterfall that cascades over native limestone and runs the length of the building.

LONGWOOD GARDENS
Rte. 1, Kennett Square, PA 19348-0501. Tel. 610.388.1000
Longwood was originally the estate of Pierre du Pont. Orangery, exhibition hall, and eighteen other conservatories.

MITCHELL PARK HORTICULTURAL CONSERVATORY, THE DOMES
524 South Layton Boulevard, Milwaukee, WI 53215. Tel. 414.649.9830
Tropical dome, arid dome, and show dome.

MOODY GARDENS
1 Hope Boulevard, Galveston, TX 77551. Tel. 1.800.582.4673
The gardens include glass houses and three ten-story glass pyramid conservatories.

NEW YORK BOTANICAL GARDENS
200th Street and Southern Boulevard, Bronx, NY 10458. Tel. 718.817.8616
Hands-on exploration of lush plantlife and biomes. Rain forest discovery stations.

PHIPPS CONSERVATORY & BOTANIAL GARDEN
One Schenley Park, Pittsburg, PA 15213. Tel. 412.622.6914
Victorian glasshouse with thirteen display rooms.

ROCKWOOD MUSEUM
610 Shipley Road, Wilmington, DE 19809. Tel. 302.761.4340
Victorian conservatory.

SAN ANTONIO BOTANICAL GARDENS
555 Kunston Place, San Antonio, TX 78209. Tel. 210.207.3263
Lucile Halsell Conservatory. Glass buildings surround a sunken courtyard and tropical lagoon.

SONNENBERG CONSERVATORY
151 Charlotte Street, Canandaigua, NY 14424. Tel. 716.394.4922
The Lord & Burnham Conservatory complex is one of the most important residential greenhouse complexes in the US.

Index

accessories 116-43
African prints 86
agate pattern tom-thumb flower pots 138
Alton Towers, gardens 11
anti-sun glass 112
antique
    French fabrics 86
    pedestal plant container 126
    shops 116
    teak chest 122
architecture 24
    elements 96-115
    embellishments 42-3
aviary conservatory 17

barbecues 30, 147
basketwork 116
beach huts and boat houses style 50
Beaumont & Fletcher, chairs 136
blinds 34-5, 91, 157
    gossamer-thin cotton 94-5
    Marston & Langinger 124-5
    natural flax 88-9
    pinoleum 46-7, 91, 113
    roof 112
brass jug 138
brasswork 82, 116
building framework 50
bulbs 129
Burton, Decimus 10

cake-stands 127, 130, 148-9
Cambridge bricks 102
candelabra 81, 85
candle holder with shade 83
canvas shades 33
Carrara statuary 143
cast-iron grilles 111
Castello di San Polo, Chianti 114
ceramics
    floors 103
    table 148-9
    tiles 73
chairs 63-4, 73-4, 76, 78, 86, 136, 146
    five-legged 63
    polished steel high-backed 73
    wicker and cane 66, 68-9, 76
chandeliers 83
Chelsea Flower Show conservatory 58-9
children's activities 18-19, 144
Chinese Room, Langley Park 20
Christmas 147, 152, 154-5
citrus fruit 129
city garden, year-round 38
climbers 119, 129
club dining room 21
coarse canvas and linens 81
coffee tables of metal and glass 76
collections display 137
colour schemes
    basic 54-5
    brilliant 92-3
    violet and buff 90
colour and texture 50-5

colours
    bright, garden room 88-9
    dark 56
    earth 56
    external 50
    green 53, 56, 56
conservatories
    builders 156
    contemporary 12
    everyday family use 18-19, 144
    new 104-5
    to upstairs terrace 38
Conservatory Plants 14
containers 129, 131, 137
copperwork 116
cork pot 123
Cotswold stonework 25
cotton prints 86
country markets 116
Crystal Palace Exhibition Hall 10
curtains 91
cycads 129

daylight and sunshine 50
decorative elements 48-95
dhurries 91
doors
    folded-back 150
    wooden 106

English willow furniture 62
entertaining and special occasions 18-19, 144, 147-54
Eugenie, Princess (passiflora) 108
evergreen plants 45, 118
exterior elements 50, 50

fabrics 50, 53, 63, 86-95, 86, 91
fanlight with leaded panes 98
fans 111, 112
ferns 132
figurative plant pot 131
fireplace 84-5, 110
    West of England stone 100
fires
    open 112
    wood 84-5
First World War 13
flagstones and cobbles 101-2
Flintham Hall, conservatory 142-3
floors 96, 100, 100-1, 103-5, 130
    and other fittings 156-7
    terracotta 91
    timber 103
    underfloor heating 111
floral print cushions 86
formal meal 151
fountains 140-2, 140, 142-3
four-seater wire bench 76
framed timber construction 24
French
    candelabra in bronze 85
    fire surround 110
    wicker chair 63
    wrought-iron chair 73
furniture 50, 62, 70-2, 76, 130, 157
    wicker 62-71, 63, 71

galvanised
    ironwork 116
    wire rack 137
garden furniture 64-5, 67, 79
gardens
    chair, navy-painted 64
    furnishing 48
    outside 38-47
    rooms
        designers, associations and courses 157-8
        evolution 8-13
        furniture 70
        plates 147
        style, elements 14-27
        table or side lights 81
        using 144-55
        views 38-47, 147
Georgian orangery 140
Gibson, Anthea, lead tub 126
glass 98-9
    buildings 50
    cake-stand 148-9
    clear and hand-blown 132
    jars 148-9
    richly coloured 99
    roofs 54-5, 138
glasshouses
    Lübbecke, Germany 39
    open to the public 158
Glenbervie, mid-century planting scheme 12
gothic
    arches 146
        windows 124-5
    garden pavilion 10
    wardian case 127
    windows and iron balcony 40
gothic-decorated, two-storey conservatory 153
gothic-pattern, wire dining chair 74
gravel 132
greenhouses 25, 129

Haddonstone grotesques 141
Hamburg, conservatory 26-7
hand-thrown clay pots 122
hanging
    baskets 119, 128
    electric lamp 83
    lamps 83
heated public glass-houses 24
heating 122
    cooling and shading 111-15
herringbone-pattern brick paving 100
hippiastrums 123
Hirsh, Susan, fabrics 53, 86
hurricane lamps 85
    on brass brackets 82

Ilford, Wiltshire, orangery 10
Indian swing 134-5
indoor
    gardening 28, 144
    plant life 17
    pool 54-5
infestations 129
inside-outside conservatory 45
interior planning 50
internal walls 50

iron
   breakfast table 76
   cake-stand plant-holders 127, 130
   chairs 74
   dining table 78
   furniture 130
Italian fountain 142-3

jardinieres 131

Kew Gardens
   Palm House 10, 24
   Sensory Garden 46-7
   veranda 31
Kibble Palace, pool 140
kilim rugs 91, 102
kitchen proximity 144

lamps 80, 82-3, 83, 85
lampshades 83
Langley Park, Chinese Room 20
lantern roof and ivy 41
large conservatory 147
lead tub 126
leafy perspectives 28-47
lean-to conservatory 52-3
light and colour 21
lighter tones 56
lighting 80-5, 137
   circuits 83
lime plaster, traditional coloured 58-9
limed-oak cricket table 77
limestone flooring 100
Lloyd Loom 63, 76, 86
Logan, Andrew, broken-mirrorwork 58
London
   lean-to conservatory 52-3
   rooftop terrace 37
   two-storey conservatory 153
long-tom pot, pyramid wire frame 122
low humidity plants 122, 156-7
low-pitched roofs 13
Lübbecke, Germany, glasshouse 39

Madeira 13
marble 100
   floor 130
Marston & Langinger
   blinds 124-5
   conservatories 16, 88-9, 98, 136, 148-9
   prints 86
   scagliola table 52-3
   Sea Green and Silver Blue paint 60-1
   wicker furniture 71
Marston, Josephine, wrought-iron table 72
Marston, Peter 50
match-boarding 96, 107
materials 21, 53, 86
mauvish-grey conservatory exterior 50
Mediterranean plants 14, 122
metal
   furniture designs 72, 76
   trellis 106, 108
mid-century planting scheme, Glenbervie 12
minimal, glass construction 51
modern conservatory 13
Moorish lantern, Fez, Morocco 82

mosaic table 72
mosaic-work 73
moveable plant stand 128
multi-surfaced planting 128
music 48

natural
   flax blinds 88-9
   light 48
   materials 53
   textures 86, 91
neutral floor 104-5
nightlights 80
nineteenth-century
   baker's rack 139
   heated public glass-houses 24
   print 137

oak-and-glass garden room 24
objects, eclectic collection 133
occasional chairs 76
ocean, terrace 32
octagonal-plan glasshouse 120-1
oil lamp with reflector 82
orangeries 10, 140, 141
Orkney pattern, wicker chair 68-9
ornaments 157
outside
   lights 83
   planting 17, 28, 51

Page, Russell 30
painted
   wall 106
   wicker 70
   wooden storage container 135
Palm House, Kew Gardens 10, 24
paper-white narcissi 123
paving 45, 100
Paxton, Joseph 10
Pennslyvania, garden room 24
Peto, H.A. 10
Phillips, Roger and Martyn Rix 14
Pinchbeck woven cotton stripe 91
pinoleum blinds 46-7, 91, 113
planting schemes 12, 28, 51, 119-31, 128
plants 119-31, 129
   containers 129, 131, 137
   cultivation 132
   holders 17, 127, 130
   jungle of 124-5
   low humidity 122, 156-7
   Mediterranean origin 14, 122
   outside 17, 28, 51
   selection 17
   suppliers 156
plastered walls 106
polished steel high-backed, chair 73
poolhouses 22-3
pools 30, 54-5, 140-1
Port Lympne, Kent, gardens 30
Portuguese candelabra 81
pots 119, 120-3, 138
pressed steel chair 146

rattan cane 70
   chairs 66

rearrangements 144
Regency period, chairs and benches 78
relaxation 144
Rhodes, Zandra, garden room 58
roofs
   blinds 112
   with carved wooden brackets 98
   glass 54-5, 138
   lantern and ivy 41
   low-pitched 13
   ventilators 114
rooftop terraces 33, 37
rough woody interior style 50
rugs 91, 102

Savannah, Georgia 30
scagliola 73
   tables 52-3, 57
Sea Green and Silver Blue paint 60-1
seats, shaped wicker benches 60-1
Sensory Garden, Kew Gardens 46-7
shades
   canvas 33
   umbrellas 30, 40
shading 111-15
shelves 132
soft furnishings 86-95, 86
Southern Spain, oil lamp with reflector 82
Spanish moss in wire basket 128
special occasions 56, 129
specialist fabrics 91
staging 132
standard lamps 80
statues 140-2, 157
steamboat gothic 30
stonework 25, 45, 100-3, 141
striped fabrics 86, 91
sunlight 50, 88-9
sunrooms 63

table cloths 86
tables 72, 76-8, 77, 144, 148-9
   and chairs 73-9
   and folded-back doors 150
   iron 76, 78
   scagliola 52-3, 57
   side and console 76
   wrought-iron 72, 75, 133
tap-and sink fountain 140
teak or iroko garden furniture 79
terraces 30-7, 32-3, 37-8
   reached through conservatory 79
terracotta 116
   flooring 91
   pots 120-1, 123, 126
   tiles 103
textures 21, 50-5, 63, 86, 91
Tilden, Philip 30
town conservatories 21
town garden 44
trellis
   and climbers 109
   metal 106, 108
   pale blue 106
   screen 36
tripod stand 130
tubs and pots 119, 126

Turkish kiosk hanging electric lamp 83
Turner, Richard 10
Tuscany sandstone 103
two-storey conservatory 153

umbrellas, shade 30, 40
underfloor heating 111
unpolished timber 73

ventilation 112, 115, 122
ventilators, roof 114
verandas 30-7, 31
Victorian
    alabaster statues 140-2
    ceramic floor 103
    conservatories 13, 17, 19
    dome 140
    winter gardens 143

Walcott Reclamation 85
walls 50, 106-7, 108-9
watering 129

waterproof lamps 83
Wedgwood plates 79
white primulas 119
wicker
    basket 123
    benches 60-1
    chairs 68-9, 76
    furniture 62-71, 63, 71
    garden furniture 64-5, 67
    lounger and footstool 64
wide beaded pine walls 107
willow 70
windows, gothic arches 124-5
wire
    baskets 128, 131
    chairs, with covered cushion 73
    dining chair, gothic-pattern 74
    four-seater bench 76
    pyramid frame 122
    rack 137
    trellis 108
wirework 116

    chairs 76
wood-boarded walls 106
wood
    doors 106
    finials 139
    flooring 103
    framed construction 24
    and glass roof 54-5
    items 98, 116, 135
    unpolished 73
    windows 106
Woods, Johanna 86
wrought-iron
    French chair 73
    tables 72, 75, 133

year-round
    city garden 38
    conservatory use 56
Yorkstone 45, 102, 103